PVC
PROJECTS
for the Outdoorsman

Building Shelters, Camping Gear, Weapons, and More Out of Plastic Pipe

PALADIN PRESS · BOULDER, COLORADO

MW01005817

Other books and videos by Tom Forbes:
Invisible Advantage: A Step-by-Step Guide to Making Ghillie Suits
    and Custom Camouflage Accessories (video)
Invisible Advantage Workbook: Ghillie Suit Construction Made Simple
Modern Muzzleloading: Black Powder Shooting for Sport,
    Survival, and Self-Defense (video)
More PVC Projects for the Outdoorsman: Building Inexpensive Shelters,
Hunting and Fishing Gear, and More Out of Plastic Pipe

PVC Projects for the Outdoorsman: Building Shelters,
    Camping Gear, Weapons, and More Out of Plastic Pipe
by Tom Forbes

Copyright © 1999 by Tom Forbes

ISBN 10: 1-58160-021-6
ISBN 13: 978-1-58160-021-6
Printed in the United States of America

Published by Paladin Press, a division of
Paladin Enterprises, Inc.
Gunbarrel Tech Center
7077 Winchester Circle
Boulder, Colorado 80301 USA
+1.303.443.7250

Direct inquiries and/or orders to the above address.

PALADIN, PALADIN PRESS, and the "horse head" design
are trademarks belonging to Paladin Enterprises and
registered in United States Patent and Trademark Office.

Visit our Web site at www.paladin-press.com

Table of Contents

Introduction

For most people, PVC pipe is found in the hardware store for one reason only—to offer an alternative to struggling with pipe-bending and soldering when replacing broken or cracked plumbing. But PVC, or polyvinyl chloride, is a durable, non-flammable plastic with too much potential to be confined to plumbing alone.

Having a passion for virtually anything associated with the outdoors, I thought to myself, "Why not make what I need for my expeditions into the wilderness myself?" I learned a long time ago—and the "C" in wood shop confirmed it—that I am not carpenter. So I decide to try working with PVC—a medium much more forgiving than wood, not to mention more affordable.

This book contains more than 30 practical pieces of outdoors equipment that can be constructed with PVC pipe. With each project we will cover the materials needed and explain how to assemble it using written instructions, photographs, and illustrations.

Chapter 1

Tools and Materials

This list will vary, but here is the most you will need to complete a basic project:
• Tape measure or yard stick
• Hack saw
• Sand paper
• Drill or electric hobby tool
• Duct tape
• Para cord
• PVC cleaner
• PVC cement or silicone chalk
• Camouflage paint or tape
• Spray foam insulation

Chapter 2

Construction Tips

Here are a few things to keep in mind during the planning and building stages:

- The projects use PVC pipe of various sizes ranging from 1/2-inch to 4 inches in diameter with end caps, elbows, T-connectors, spacers, and reducers. As a general rule, use the heavy-walled PVC pipe for these projects.
- Use PVC cleaner on pipe surfaces that will be cemented.
- These projects can be painted, but be sure to choose a paint that will work on plastic. If you wish to camouflage your PVC pipe, camouflage tape works very well as an alternative to painting.
- Parts used for some projects may not be readily available. In these cases you may have to get a bit inventive. For example, several projects use a three-way 90-degree elbow that is the same diameter on all ends. These can sometimes be hard to find. Should this be the case, you can get by using the same style of elbow that is threaded on the third opening and attaching a threaded end onto the PVC pipe.
- The best way to determine whether or not to cement a project is to decide how portable it needs to be. Many projects, such as the shelters, can be left uncemented or partially

5

cemented to allow for easy disassembly. In others, most notably the snowshoes and the sled, cementing the finished project is essential.

- As you shop for supplies, you'll notice that there are different styles of end caps. Generally, smaller caps are flat, while the larger (4-inch) caps are domed. In some projects, either will do, but in others, such as the drinking cup and the water bucket, you must use flat end caps.

- In projects that use nylon rope or para cord, you can secure the knots by heating them with a match or a lighter.

- Several projects, such as the ice grippers, tent poles, and walking stick, call for an end cap to be fitted with a nail. Use a roofing nail, or other type with a wide enough head so that the edges of the head will be secured between the end of the PVC pipe and the bottom of the end cap. If the nail head is too small, a washer can be placed on top of it to hold it in place.

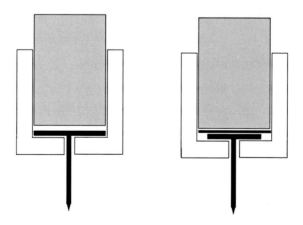

Ideally, use a nail with a head wide enough to fit between the end of the pipe and the end cap (left). If that is not possible, place a washer on top of the nail head (right) to brace it against the pipe.

Chapter 3

Shelters

Food, shelter, and clothing are man's most basic needs, but only one can be made from PVC. Whether it is for protection from the rain or just a little privacy, having a shelter can make a stay in the wilderness much more comfortable.

These PVC shelters are lightweight for easy portability, simple to construct and inexpensive to build.

Teepee

Teepees are dependable shelters that can be put together quickly. This one can act as a shelter for one person or as a place to store supplies out of the weather.

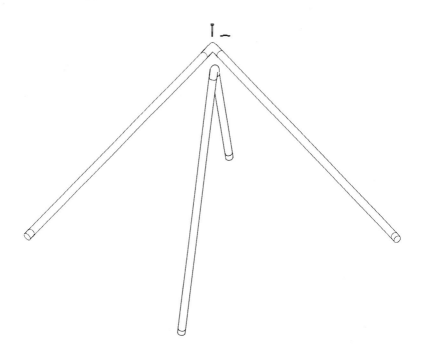

Materials:
- Four 8-foot lengths of 2-inch diameter pipe
- Two 2-inch diameter 90-degree elbows
- Four 2-inch diameter end caps
- One 6-inch long, 1/2-inch diameter bolt w/wing nut
- Two 8-foot-square tarps
- 24 feet of para cord
- Duct tape

Instructions:

Step 1

Insert the 8-foot pipes into the elbows. The pipes will serve as the supports, or legs, of the teepee. Stand the two A-frame supports upright, then overlap the elbows at the top. The legs of the A-frame should extend in four directions.

Step 2

Find the center of the overlapping elbows and drill a 1/2-inch hole through both elbows. Then insert the 6-inch bolt from the bottom of the elbows and secure it with the wing nut.

Step 3

Measure the distance from the bottom of the legs on the overlapping A-frame to the ground and cut this difference off the other two legs. This will provide four legs of equal length, making a level and stable structure. After trimming, snap on the end caps.

Step 4

Tie the tarp to the pipes by looping a rope through the grommets. Leave a small opening at the top for ventilation.

Plastic sheeting can be used for a cover or to make a pattern for heavier material. Duct tape or para cord can be used to secure the tarp. For a more form-fitting cover, tape the excess material up rather than cutting it. This will help the cover maintain its strength and make it less apt to tear.

Lean-To

One of the easiest and most useful projects in this book has to be the lean-to. It provides quick and reliable shelter for the outdoorsman.

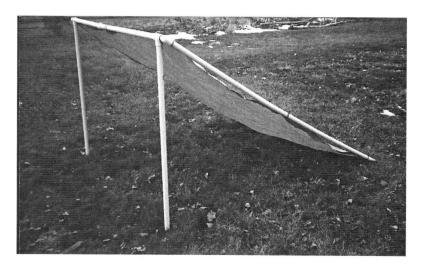

A PVC-pipe lean-to can protect you and your gear from the elements. (Photo by Scout Forbes.)

Materials:
- Two 8-foot lengths of 1-inch diameter pipe
- One 6-foot length of 1-inch diameter pipe
- Two 4-foot lengths of 1-inch diameter pipe
- Two reduced 1-inch diameter 90-degree elbows
- Two 1-inch diameter T-connectors
- One 6-by-8-foot or larger tarp
- 20 feet of para cord

Instructions:

Step 1
Mark the 4-foot pipes four inches from the ends and cut them diagonally from this mark to the bottoms of the pipes, forming points.

Step 2

Attach a T-connector to each end of the 6-foot pipe. Then attach the 4-foot pipes to the bottom ends of each T-connector and sink them into the ground.

Step 3

Attach an elbow to each of the 8-foot pipes. Insert the reduced end into the remaining opening of each T-connector. Adjust the angles of the 8-foot pipes so that the ends reach the ground.

Step 4

Use the para cord to attach the tarp by tying it to the lean-to frame. By using a larger tarp, such as one that's 18-by-14-foot, you can totally enclose the shelter.

Portable Ground Blind

A portable and lightweight blind can be real handy when the terrain doesn't supply the cover you need. This design adapts easily to changes in size and shape. For this project, the blind will be a small one—4-foot-square.

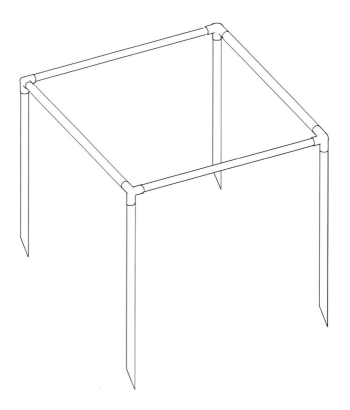

Materials:
- Eight 4-foot lengths of 3/4-inch diameter pipe
- Four 3/4-inch diameter three-way 90-degree elbows
- One 4-by-16-foot piece of camouflage material (camo net or a camo print.)
- Sixteen curtain-hanging clips

- Subdued-color spray paint
- Spray foam insulation

Instructions:

Step 1

Select four 4-foot pipes. Slide four curtain clips onto each one. Paint clips before assembly, if desired.

Step 2

Insert the four pipes into the top openings on the elbows, forming a square.

Step 3

The remaining pipes will form the legs of the blind. Mark the pipes three inches from the ends. Using a saw or hobby tool, cut the pipes from the marks to the ends of the pipes at angles to form points.

Step 4

Fill each of these pipes with spray foam. The foam will help keep dirt from filling the pipes when they're pushed into the ground.

Step 5

Attach the pipes to the bottom opening on each elbow.

Step 6

Push the sharpened end of the pipes into the ground, then attach the camouflage material to the clips.

Latrine/Shower Screen

When taking a shower or answering the call of nature, it's nice to have a little bit of privacy. The latrine/shower screen can provide just that.

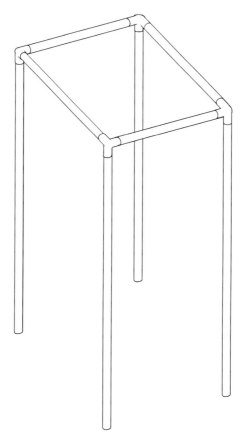

Materials:
- Four 6-foot lengths of 1-inch diameter pipe
- Four 3-foot lengths of 1-inch diameter pipe
- Four 1-inch diameter three-way 90-degree elbows
- One 8-by-12-foot tarp
- 16 feet of para cord

Instructions:

Step 1

Insert a 6-foot pipe into the bottom opening of each elbow to form the vertical supports.

Step 2

Insert the 3-foot pipes into the remaining openings on the elbows to form a square. These will be your lateral braces.

Step 3

Run the para cord through the grommet loops on the tarp. With a spiral wrap, hang the tarp from the lateral braces.

To help keep the entrance shut, tie a rock to the bottom loop to weight the tarp.

Chapter 4

Camping Gear

Though it's true we live in a modern age of instant gratification, many people still find pleasure in building things themselves and getting away from civilization now and then. Creating your own camping gear combines these pursuits. And while the use of PVC doesn't exactly qualify as living off the land, it does make the construction of outdoors equipment easy and affordable.

Cot Frame

Cots can make sleeping much more comfortable, but they are usually heavy and awkward to carry. A sturdy, lightweight cot can be constructed of PVC pipe and a surplus cot cover.

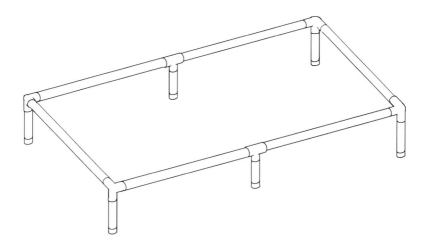

Materials:
- Four 3-foot lengths of 2-inch diameter pipe
- Two 28-inch lengths of 2-inch diameter pipe
- Six 6-inch lengths of 2-inch diameter pipe
- Four 2-inch diameter three-way 90-degree elbows
- Two 2-inch diameter T-connectors
- Six 2-inch diameter end caps
- One cot cover

Instructions:

Step 1
Insert the four 3-foot pipes into the loops on the sides of the cot cover. Then insert the two 28-inch pieces into the loops at the head and foot of the cot.

Step 2
Attach an elbow to each 3-foot pipe at each corner.

Step 3
Join the open ends of the 3-foot pipes with the T-connectors.

Step 4
Insert the ends of the 28-inch pipes into the openings on the elbows.

Step 5
Turn the cot frame over and insert the six 6-inch pieces into the bottom openings of the T-connectors and elbows and place the caps on the ends.

If you do not have access to a cot canvas, try lawn chair webbing and pop rivet it into place. You can leave this project uncemented for portability.

Portable Table

Because of their size and weight, tables are often impractical to take along for use outdoors. This light, portable table will make spending time outdoors much more comfortable by supplying you with a platform to keep things up off the ground, to eat from, or even a place to play cards.

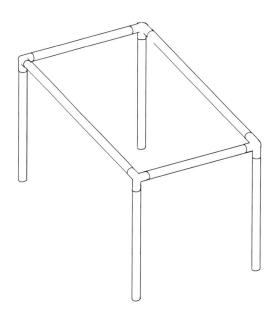

Materials:
- Six 18-inch lengths of 1-inch diameter pipe
- Two 24-inch lengths of 1-inch diameter pipe
- Four 1-inch diameter three-way 90-degree elbows
- One 18-by-24-inch piece of cardboard or similar material

Instructions:

Step 1

Insert one 18-inch pipe into the bottom opening of each elbow.

Step 2

Form the short sides of the rectangular table by connecting two pairs of elbows with the two remaining 18-inch pipes.

Step 3

Using the 24-inch pipes, connect the elbows to form the table frame.

Step 4

Lay the table top on the frame.

The table top can be secured by attaching snaps onto the frame and the top, or by attaching a series of web straps with snaps that wrap around the frame.

Emergency Tent Poles

Go on enough camping trips and sooner or later you are going to end up with a bent or broken tent pole. This can be remedied quickly and affordably by using a piece of pipe.

Materials:
- One 1/2-inch diameter pipe (cut to desired length)
- Two 1/2-inch diameter end caps
- Two nails

Instructions:

Step 1
Cut the pipe to the desired length.

Step 2

Drill a hole in the center of an end cap, then insert a nail from the inside of the cap so that the pointed portion of the nail is exposed. This nail will go through the grommet on the tent fabric. Most times only one end will need a nail; the other end can simply be capped.

Step 3

Place the caps on the pipes.

Some modern tents use an external support to hold up the tent. These can be made using PVC pipe and one or more 90- or 45-degree elbows. Use the existing supports as a guide.

Waterproof Toilet Paper Holder

A friend of mine once told me that there were three things he could not stand: "Second lieutenants, cold coffee, and wet toilet paper." There is nothing we can do about the first one. The second we may have some control over, but (no pun intended) the third one we can control!

Materials:
- One 18-inch length of 4-inch diameter pipe
- Two 4-inch diameter end caps
- PVC cement

Instructions:

Step 1
  Cement one end cap to the pipe.

Step 2
  Insert toilet paper rolls and simply snap on the other end cap.

This will hold 4 rolls of standard toilet paper. If that much is not needed, then either make it shorter or use the vacant space for other toiletries.

Drinking Cup

A sturdy drinking cup is a simple, useful item to have on hand on a camping trip.

Materials:
• One 5-inch length of 2- or 3-inch diameter pipe.
• One 2- or 3-inch diameter end cap

Instructions:

Step 1
    Determine the diameter cup that you want and cut a 5-inch piece of pipe. Cap one end and cement it in place. Use a flat cap for this project, not a domed one.

Step 2
    Use sand paper to smooth the rough or sharp edges of the open end, then thoroughly wash out the cup.

Water Bucket

This little bucket works well for hauling small quantities of water. The bucket made here holds approximately one liter.

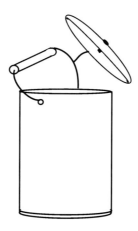

Materials:
- One 8-inch length of 4-inch diameter pipe
- One 4-inch length of 1/2-inch diameter pipe
- Two 4-inch diameter end caps
- 16 inches of para cord
- PVC cement

Instructions:

Step 1
    Cement an end cap to the bottom of the 8-inch pipe. Now drill two holes 1/2-inch down from the top on opposite sides. These holes will be used for the handle cords.

Step 2
    Drill a hole into the center of the second end cap.

Step 3

Cut a 4-inch piece of the para cord. Make a knot at one end and run the other end of it through the hole from the inside.

Step 4

Run the 12-inch para cord through the 1/2-inch diameter pipe. This pipe will serve as the handle. Push the ends of the para cord through the two holes at the top of the bucket and knot them on the inside. Heat knots to secure.

Step 5

Tie the 4-inch para cord to the 12-inch cord and you have a lid that will stay with the bucket. Do not cement this one or you will have a permanent lid.

Match/Cigarette Case

This particular case will hold more than 50 wooden matches or a pack of cigarettes. It can be made with or without the para cord lanyard.

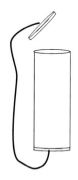

Materials:
- One 4-inch length of 1 1/2-inch diameter pipe
- Two 1 1/2-inch diameter end caps
- 8 inches of para cord
- PVC cement

Instructions:

Step 1
   Drill a 1/4-inch hole in each end cap. Knot one end of the para cord and run it through the hole of one cap so that the knot is on the underside of the cap. Run the loose end of the para cord through the top of the second cap, also knotting it on the underside. Using silicone chalk or PVC cement, seal the holes on both sides of the caps.

Step 2
   Sand both ends of the pipe and attach one end cap with PVC cement. Be sure not to cement the lid.

Walking Stick

The walking stick is a terrific project. It does not require many materials and can be real handy for weekend treks.

Materials:
- One shoulder-height 3/4-inch diameter pipe
- Two 3/4-inch diameter end caps
- One nail or field arrow point
- 12 inches of heating-pipe insulation or a foam bicycle handle cover
- 18 inches of para cord
- Duct tape

Instructions:

Step 1
Determine the length of the walking stick by holding the pipe to the top of your shoulder. At this point, mark it and cut it.

Step 2
Slide the piece of insulation or foam over the top and down the pipe until 1/2-inch of the pipe is exposed at the top end. To prevent the padding from sliding down the staff, make several wraps with duct tape just below the padding.

Step 3
Mark the pipe between the end cap and the padding and drill a 1/4-inch hole through both sides. Then roll up a piece of sand paper or emery cloth and sand the hole, removing any sharp edges. Insert the para cord through the hole and knot it.

Step 4
Cement the top end cap. Drill a hole through the other end cap and insert the nail and attach the cap to the bottom of the stick.

Pack Frame

An inexpensive way to carry your gear into parts unknown is to construct your own pack frame. This one is lightweight and surprisingly durable. It can be used as a pack board or with the ALICE pack.

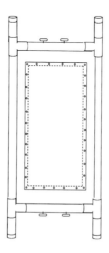

Materials:
- Two 24-inch lengths of 3/4-inch diameter pipe
- Two 12-inch lengths of 3/4-inch diameter pipe
- Four 4-inch lengths of 3/4-inch diameter pipe
- Four 3/4-inch diameter T-connectors
- Four 3/4-inch diameter end caps
- One piece of canvas, about 11-by-22-inches
- 12 feet of para cord
- Four picture-hanging brackets
- Two 3-foot lengths of 1 inch webbing
- Pop rivets
- Duct tape

Instructions:

Step 1
Drill four holes through both 12-inch pipes to accommodate the brackets. Measure it so the brackets are a couple of inches apart and centered.

Step 2
Place a piece of duct tape over the rough edges of the brackets. Pop-rivet the brackets to each 12-inch pipe. Webbing attached to these brackets will keep the shoulder straps from sliding on the pipe.

Step 3
Slide the bottom openings of the T-connectors over each end of each 12-inch pipe. Create a rectangle by inserting the 24-inch pipes into the sides of the T-connectors.

Step 4
Insert the 4-inch pipes into the remaining hole of each T-connector and add end caps

Step 5
Prepare the canvas by folding a 1/2-inch seam on all four sides. Glue or sew the seam. Once the seam is finished, begin at one of the corners and make marks two inches apart directly in the middle of the seam. At each of these marks punch a hole big enough for a piece of para cord to go through. With the holes punched in the canvas, lay the canvas in the center of the frame rectangle.

Step 6
Begin lacing the para cord through the canvas and around the pipe frame. Be sure not to lace it too tight, and keep the canvas centered. Once you have laced the cord around the frame, tie it off with a secure knot.

Step 7

Run the two pieces of webbing through the picture brackets and adjust the straps for fit. ALICE-pack straps will work well.

Travois

The travois is one of man's oldest methods of transportation and can be pulled by a horse, dog, or man. It allows one to carry additional gear without having the weight directly on the body.

Transporting supplies can be a drag in the outdoors, but this easy-to-make travois can keep the extra weight off your shoulders. (Photo by Scout Forbes.)

Materials:
- Two 6-foot lengths of 1-inch diameter pipe
- Four 18-inch lengths of 1-inch diameter pipe
- 12 feet of para cord
- Webbing (optional)

Instructions:

Step 1
Mark four holes on each 6-foot pipe. Start 6 inches from the

bottom and make the first mark, then make the next three marks six inches apart. Drill each hole all the way through the pipe.

Step 2

Make a mark 1/2-inch from each end on the 18-inch pipes and drill a hole through one side only.

Step 3

To lash the 18-inch pipes to the support poles, make a large knot in the para cord and start by running it up through the bottom hole of a 6-foot pipe. Once through, push the cord through the first hole of an 18-inch pipe. Run the cord through the 18-inch pipe and out the second hole and through both sides of the corresponding hole in the 6-foot pipe.

Step 4

Continue this process until all of the 18-inch pipes are lashed to the 6-foot pipes and tie the cord off.

To make the task of pulling the travois easier you may attach a strip of webbing near where your hands hold the travois. The webbing can be placed across the shoulders to help take some of the weight off your arms. Other options include making a harness for a dog or horse, if available.

Carrying Pole

The carrying pole is no doubt one of the easiest projects to construct. It can be used, as it has been for centuries, to carry game or supplies. Its simplicity allows for several practical improvements without any hassle. Adding padding to the pole will substantially increase the comfort level of carrying weight on your shoulders. Putting I-bolts in the pole and using snap links will allow you to attach or detach your load quickly, as well as prevent it from sliding up and down the pole over uneven terrain.

Materials:
- One 8-foot length of 2-inch diameter pipe
- Two 3-inch #10 I-bolts
- Two snap links
- Two 12-inch-square pieces of foam rubber
- Duct tape.

Instructions:

Step 1
    Begin by drilling two holes through the pipe, one about 16 inches from each end.

Step 2

Insert the I-bolts and secure them with the nuts. Then attach the snap links.

Step 3

Wrap the foam rubber around the ends of the pipe and secure it with duct tape.

Chapter 5

Winter Sports

Part of the excitement of winter activities is the challenge that both the sport and the elements provide. Making your own sled and other snow gear adds to the fun. If you've ever spent a snowy day cooped up in the house with nothing to do, you'll appreciate having one of these projects waiting in your workshop.

Sled

Needless to say, living in South Dakota has given me lots of experience with snow. And being so well acquainted with it, I thought it only logical to make a sled for hauling my gear.

Materials:

Top View

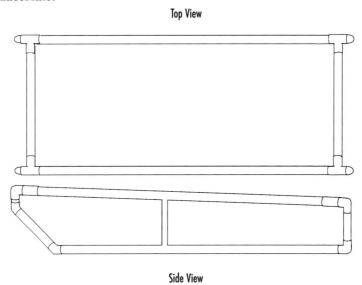

Side View

- Two 48-inch lengths of 1-inch diameter pipe
- Two 46-inch lengths of 1-inch diameter pipe
- Two 18 1/2-inch lengths of 1-inch diameter pipe
- Two 9-inch lengths of 1-inch diameter pipe
- Two 9-inch lengths of 1/2-inch diameter CPVC pipe
- Two 6-inch lengths of 1-inch diameter pipe
- Two 2-inch lengths of 1-inch diameter pipe
- Four 1-inch diameter 45-degree elbows
- Two 1-inch diameter 90-degree elbows
- Four 1-inch diameter reduced 90-degree elbows
- Four 1-inch diameter T-connectors
- Two 2-inch long I-bolts

Hauling equipment and supplies over snowy ground is easier with a lightweight PVC-pipe sled. (Photo by Scout Forbes.)

- Two 2-foot lengths of nylon boat rope.
- One tarp, approximately 48-by-18-inches.

Instructions:

Step 1
Due to the amount of pieces used in this project, it will be very helpful to label everything.

Step 2
Attach a T-connector to each end of each 48-inch pipe. Join these pipes by inserting an 18 1/2-inch pipe into the bottom of each T-connector. This should create a long rectangle with T-connectors on the corners. This will be the top platform of the sled. Set it aside while you complete the runners.

Note: There are two ways to attach the tarp to the top of the sled. You can fold and sew the tarp's edges and create sleeves to run the pipes through, or you can snap grommets along the edge of the tarp and attach it to the frame with rope. If you choose the first method, it should be done before the sled is completely assembled.

Step 3

Attach a 90-degree elbow onto the end of each 46-inch pipe. This will become the rear of the sled. At the other end of each 46-inch pipe attach a 45-degree elbow. This will become the front of the sled.

Step 4

At the rear of the sled, insert a 6-inch pipe into the opening of each 90-degree elbow. Then attach a reduced-90-degree elbow to the top of each 6-inch pipe.

Step 5

At the front of the sled, insert a 9-inch pipe into each 45-degree elbow. With this done, attach a second 45-degree elbow to the end of each 9-inch pipe. Insert 2-inch spacers into the open elbow ends. Attach a reduced 90-degree elbow to the top of each spacer. With this done, you have built the runners.

Step 6

Drill a 9/16-inch hole on the top side of each of the 46-inch pipes (your runners) 21 1/2 inches from the front of the rear 90-degree elbow. Be sure not to drill through both sides of the pipe. With this done, insert the 9-inch CPVC support pipe into the hole. Now drill a corresponding hole into each 48-inch pipe 19 inches from the front of the rear T-connector. The side with the hole will become the bottom of the platform.

Step 7

Attach the platform to the runners by lining up the holes for the 9-inch CPVC pipes and inserting them into the platform on each side. Insert the reduced 90-degree elbows into the open ends of the T-connectors on each corner. Since you'll be forcing the top platform to angle upwards slightly at the front of the sled, you may have to put some elbow grease into this step.

Step 8

Drill holes into the 90-degree elbows at the front of the sled. Insert the I-bolts and screw them into place. Attach the rope.

Snow shoes

The benefits of using snowshoes are quite obvious if you have ever had to travel any distance in deep snow. These shoes, though not designed for long-range arctic travel, will serve their purpose well for short treks.

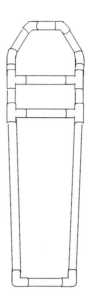

Materials for one shoe:
- Two 24-inch lengths of 1/2-inch diameter pipe
- Two 9-inch lengths of 1/2-inch diameter pipe
- One 6 1/2-inch length of 1/2-inch diameter pipe
- Two 6-inch lengths of 1/2-inch diameter pipe
- One 5 1/4-inch length of 1/2-inch diameter pipe
- Two 4-inch lengths of 1/2-inch diameter pipe
- Two 3-inch lengths of 1/2-inch diameter pipe
- Four 1/2-inch diameter 45-degree elbows
- Two 1/2-inch diameter 90-degree elbows
- Four 1/2-inch diameter T-connectors
- Webbing or strips of heavy inner tube

- PVC cement
- Pop rivets or small screws

Instructions:

Step 1

Begin by assembling the center portion, which will support your foot. First, join the sides of two T-connectors with a 4-inch pipe. Repeat with the other two T-connectors and 4-inch pipe.

Step 2

Form a rectangle by inserting a 9-inch pipe into the downward opening of each T-connector. Insert the 24-inch pipes into the open ends of the T-connectors on one side of the rectangle.

Step 3

Attach a 90-degree elbow onto the bottom of each 24-inch pipe. Insert the 6 1/2-inch pipe into the open ends of the 90-degree elbows to close off the back of the shoe.

Step 4

Attach the 3-inch pipes to the open ends of the T-connectors on the rectangle. Now attach a 45-degree elbow to the end of each 3-inch pipe. Insert a 6-inch pipe into the open end of the elbow. Do not cement these joints yet.

Step 5

Attach the 45-degree elbows to the 6-inch pipes. Connect the elbows and finish off the toe with the 5 1/4 inch pipe. Do not cement these joints yet.

Step 6

To create a lift to the front of the snowshoe, rotate the 45-degree elbows closest to the center area upwards until they stop. Now rotate the 45-degree elbows at the tip of the shoe downwards until they stop. The toe should now be higher than the rest of the shoe. Take a permanent marker and draw a line across the elbow onto the pipes. Disassemble the parts just marked and then cement them together, lining up the marks.

Step 7
With the frame constructed, you can now attach the webbing. The webbing material can be just about anything your imagination will conjure up. Just make sure it is light and durable. Lace the webbing across the frame and secure to frame. The webbing can be secured with either pop rivets or small screws.

Ice-Fishing Pole

Ice fishing is a sport that has been popular in the north country for years. Part of its popularity is due to how inexpensive it is to get into.

Materials:
- One 24-inch length of 1/2-inch diameter pipe
- Two 1/2-inch diameter end caps
- One 3-inch long nail
- One small I-screw
- One cork
- Fishing line
- Two 2-inch lengths of 1/4-inch diameter wooden dowel
- PVC cement

Instructions:

Step 1
Determine which end of the pole will be the bottom and have the nail to secure the pole to the ice. With the nail end determined, measure two inches up from the bottom. Drill a very small hole and insert the I-screw.

Step 2

Measure two inches up from the I-screw and drill a second hole 1/4-inch in diameter. Drill a third hole 10 inches above the second. Insert a dowel into each hole and cement into place.

Step 3

Drill a hole into one of the end caps and insert the nail from the inside. Cement this end cap onto the bottom and cement the other end cap on the top of the pole. Push the cork over the nail when the pole is not in use.

Step 4

Tie the fishing line to the lower dowel and run the line through the I-screw. Begin to wrap the fishing line around the two dowels. When you have enough string on the dowels, place your weight and hook on and hang up your "Gone fishin' " sign!

Ice-Fishing Tip-Up

This little gadget allows you to watch several ice-fishing holes at the same time. Place the long pipes of the tip-up over the hole and balance it for each fish strike. When a fish bites, the tip-up will rotate and the flag will go up. Though not built for monster bass, it will work well for crappie, perch, or small walleye.

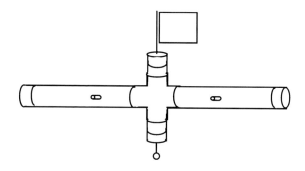

Materials:
- Two 8-inch lengths of 1/2-inch diameter pipe
- Two 2-inch lengths of 1/2-inch diameter pipe
- One 1/2-inch diameter four-way T-connector
- Four 1/2-inch diameter end caps
- One steel fishing leader
- One 1/2-inch long 1/8-inch diameter steel pin
- One marking flag
- One 1-inch length of 5/8-inch diameter wooden dowel rod
- Two 1 1/2-inch lengths of 1/4-inch diameter wooden dowel rods
- PVC cement

Instructions:

Step 1
Insert the two 8-inch pipes into the four-way T-connector directly across from one another and place an end cap on each.

Step 2

Insert the two 2-inch pipes into the remaining holes in the T-connector.

Step 3

Place the 1-inch dowel rod into one of the 2-inch pipes. Place an end cap over it. Then drill a small hole through both the end cap and the tip of the dowel rod. Insert a marking flag and cement it into place.

Step 4

Drill a 3/16-inch diameter hole in the remaining end cap and insert the steel leader into the hole. Run the steel pin through the eyelet of the leader and attach the cap to the 2-inch pipe opposite the flag.

Step 5

Drill 1/4-inch diameter holes in the 8-inch pipes on each side of the T-connector and insert a 1 1/2-inch dowel rod into each one and cement them into place. You will wrap your fishing line around these rods.

Ice-Grip Handles

If you fall through the ice, the immediate problem becomes pulling yourself out. Obviously you get soaked, and as you try to pull yourself out your hands can slip. Wearing these handles around your neck will make them easy to reach and use to pull yourself to safety. The corks can be pulled off with your teeth but most often that's not necessary, as they should give enough or disintegrate when plunged into the ice.

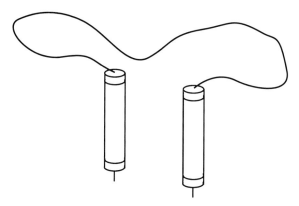

Materials:
- Two 6-inch lengths of 1/2-inch diameter pipe
- Four 1/2-inch diameter end caps
- Two roofing nails
- 36 inches of para cord
- Two corks

Instructions:

Step 1
Drill a 1/4-inch hole through each of the end caps.

Step 2
Run the para cord through the tops of two of the end caps and tie a large knot on the inside of each. Then attach these end caps to the tops of the 6-inch pipes

Step 3

Slide a roofing nail through both of the remaining end caps and slide these caps onto the bottoms of the 6-inch pipes. Cement all four end caps. Finally, stick a cork on the end of each nail to protect yourself.

Chapter 6

Water Sports

Being lightweight and watertight when properly sealed, PVC pipe is a natural material for a variety of projects for use in and around the water.

Equipment Raft

For years I figured there had to be an easier way to drag traps and decoys through waist-deep water than tugging an unruly john boat. Well, my prayers have been answered. This neat little craft will make the task of loading and unloading from a vehicle—not to mention launching and retrieving—much easier. The raft we are building here will be 4 feet long. I would not recommend going much over that because then you are back to the problems mentioned above. This raft is not to be used for people—it is strictly intended for equipment.

Materials:
- Two 4-foot lengths of 4-inch diameter pipe
- Four 4-inch diameter end caps

- Two 1 1/2-inch I-bolts w/nuts
- About 24 inches of para cord, cut into four sections
- One 6-foot length of nylon boat rope
- Spray foam insulation
- One 3-inch diameter steel ring
- One 44-by-24-inch piece of treated 1/4-inch plywood or plastic material
- Two rubber washers

Instructions:

Step 1

Start by drilling eight 1/4-inch holes in the plywood. At each corner, drill one hole that is one inch from the edges on both sides, and a second hole 3 inches or so toward the center of the board. See illustration for placement.

Step 2

Run a piece of para cord through each pair of holes, leaving the loose ends on top. Allow loops underneath large enough to accommodate the 4-foot pipe.

Step 3

Drill a hole into the centers of two of the end caps. Insert the I-bolt from the outside of the cap. Place a rubber washer on the end and secure the bolt with the nut.

Step 4

Cap one end of each 4-foot pipe with an I-bolted cap and fill it with spray foam. After a few seconds the foam will set up and you can cap the other end.

Step 5

Now slide the capped pipe through the cord loops under the plywood. Pull the loops tight and tie them off.

Step 6

Run the nylon boat rope through the I-bolts and tie the remaining rope to the ring. This will allow you to pull the raft more easily.

Buoy

This simple little gadget is without a doubt one of my favorites. It gives divers, fishermen, and others having a need for a marker in the water an inexpensive alternative to store-bought buoys. It can even be set up with a small light or chemical stick.

Materials:
- One 14-inch length of 4-inch diameter pipe
- One 2-inch length of 1/2-inch diameter pipe
- Two 4-inch diameter end caps
- One 1/4-inch I-bolt with nut
- Spray foam insulation
- One length of nylon cord with weight
- PVC cement

Instructions:

Step 1

Drill a 1/4-inch hole in one of the end caps and insert the I-bolt from the outside of the cap and secure with the nut.

Step 2

Cement this end cap onto the 14-inch pipe. This will be the bottom.

Step 3

Spray the foam insulation into the pipe and let it set up. If the foam expands over the top just shave it off with a knife.

Step 4

Drill a 9/16-inch hole in the top of the other end cap. Then insert the 1/2-inch diameter pipe into the end cap and cement it into place.

Step 5

Cement the remaining end cap on the pipe.

Step 6

Now you can attach the nylon cord and weight. Insert a chemical stick into the 1/2-inch pipe at the other end to mark your buoy at night.

Fishing-Rod Holder

The fishing-rod holder is a device for the shore fisherman or woman who likes to use more than one rod. It lets you set up one rod for fishing off the bottom while you try out your favorite crank bait.

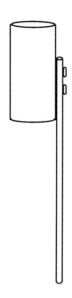

Materials:
• One 6-inch length of 2-inch diameter pipe
• One 14-inch length of 1/4- or 1/2-inch diameter steel rod
• Two pop rivets or 1/4-inch bolts with nuts.

Instructions:

Step 1
Drill two 1/4-inch holes halfway down the length of the pipe 2 inches apart.

Step 2

Drill two corresponding holes in the steel rod.

Step 3

Match up the holes in the pipe with the holes in the steel rod and either pop rivet them or bolt them together. If you use the bolts, put the heads on the inside of the pipe and attach the nuts on the outside of the steel rod. This will be easier on the fishing rod handle when it's in the holder.

Step 4

Sharpen the long end of the steel rod with a file or a grinding wheel to make it easier to stick into the ground.

Chapter 7

Archery

Bows and arrows must be stored and transported with great care to avoid breakage. These cases will protect your gear from unruly pack horses and uncaring baggage handlers, so whether you are going on a hunt or to the tournament of a lifetime, you'll arrive with your equipment in perfect condition.

Hard Bow Case

A hard bow case for either a longbow or recurve bow can be built with PVC pipe. The bow's individual design and length will determine the size of the case. For this particular project we will build a simple hard case for a longbow.

Materials:
- One 64-inch length of 3-inch diameter pipe
- Two 3-inch diameter end caps
- Two gun-sling swivels, bases and screws
- One nylon gun sling
- Foam rubber
- Glue

Instructions:

Step 1
Drill two holes in the 64-inch pipe, the first one approximately one foot from the top and the other approximately 2 feet from the first hole.

Step 2
Screw in the sling swivel bases and attach the swivels and sling.

Step 3
Glue a piece of foam into each of the end caps. Cement the bottom end cap in place.

Step 4
Insert your bow and place the end cap on and you're ready to go.

Be sure the pipe is long enough so that it does not place stress on the bow limbs when the cap is on. The foam should merely help hold the bow in place.

Arrow case

One thing often overlooked by archers and bowhunters is protecting their arrows. Many times I have left arrows in a bow quiver figuring they would be safe, only to find that something fell on them or the bow tipped over and bent or broke several of them. This case is real handy for storage or transportation.

Materials:
- One 30-inch length of 4-inch diameter pipe
- Two 4-inch diameter end caps
- Two pieces of foam rubber
- Dowel rods
- Permanent marker
- Glue

Instructions:

Step 1
Glue a piece of foam rubber to an end cap.

Step 2
Place the second piece of foam rubber over the first piece, but do not glue it. Heat an old screwdriver or comparable piece of steel. Insert the heated screwdriver into the two pieces of foam, melting a slot for each arrow to be stored. Be sure to leave some room around each hole. Remove the second piece of foam.

Step 3
Cement the end cap with the foam rubber to the bottom of the pipe.

Step 4
Glue the second piece of foam rubber to the remaining end cap. Using several long dowel rods, line up the holes in the foam pieces. Then take a permanent marker and mark the pipe and cap

to ensure that the foam will always be lined up and that each arrow will go into an individual hole. By doing this you not only protect the shaft but also the fletching.

Chapter 8

Firearms

Target shooters and hunters are often forced to travel great distances to find ranges and hunting areas, so portability is a big consideration when choosing shooting gear. Having lightweight, easily packed equipment can make the trip a lot smoother.

Target holder

The neat thing about this target holder is that it can be built and cemented together, or left uncemented to be disassembled for storage and transportation.

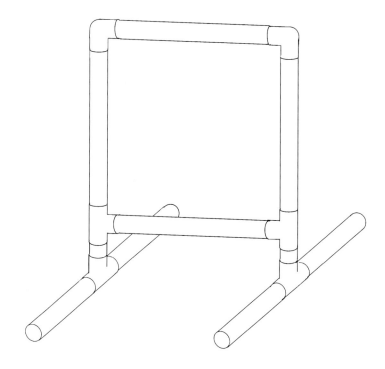

Materials:
- Four 24-inch lengths of 1-inch diameter pipe
- Four 12-inch lengths of 1-inch diameter pipe
- Two 2-inch lengths of 1-inch diameter pipe
- Two 1-inch diameter 90-degree elbows
- Four 1-inch diameter end caps
- Four 1-inch diameter T-connectors
- Four alligator clips
- PVC cement

Instructions:

Step 1

Drill two holes into two of the 24-inch pipes. The holes should be 4 inches from each end of the pipe. Insert the alligator clips and cement them in place. These pipes will serve as the top and bottom bars of the target holder and the clips will hold the paper target.

Step 2
Attach the bottom openings of two T-connectors to the ends of one of the alligator-clipped 24-inch pipes. Then insert the two unclipped 24-inch pipes into the tops of each T-connector.

Step 3
Attach an elbow to the ends of the unclipped 24-inch pipes, and insert the second alligator-clipped 24-inch pipe between them, making a square.

Step 4
Insert the 2-inch pipes into open ends of the T-connectors. Attach the remaining T-connectors to the 2-inch pipes.

Step 5
Make feet for the stand by attaching the four 12-inch pipes into the ends of the T-connectors and capping them.

Fill the feet with sand or lead shot to provide weight and help to keep the target holder in place.

Speed Loader

I grew up hunting rabbits with a tube-feed .22-caliber bolt-action rifle. It was a good rifle, but loading it required removing the bullets from a paper box and sliding them into the loading port on the tube. Easy enough in the summer, but not so easy in the winter when your fingers are cold. A friend and I figured it was much easier to take cartridges out of the box at home and put them into speed loaders. To top off the magazine we just pulled the inner magazine tube out and poured the rounds in. First we tried for maximum fire power—15-round tubes—but these proved too long and did not fit well into coat pockets. So we settled on 5 rounds. They take up a little more room, but are still very handy.

Materials:
- One 5-inch length of 1/2-inch diameter CPVC pipe
- Two 1/2-inch diameter CPVC end caps.

Instructions:

Step 1

Place an end cap on the pipe and insert the rounds.

Step 2

Attach the other end cap and color or somehow mark it so that you know which is the bullet end and which is the case end. That way, when it come time to load your rifle you know which end to open and pour down the tube.

Important: This is to be used only with rimfire ammunition. Do not use this with spitzer or centerfire cartridges.

Shooting Rests

Shooting rests can be constructed using two different methods. One is a monopod once used by the Japanese, and the other is the cross-stick method often used by the buffalo hunters. Both provide the shooter with a relatively stable shooting platform.

Monopod shooting rests made of PVC pipe are easily portable and take up little space. Here, the author uses the rest to take aim with his .50-caliber Hatfield Kentucky long rifle. (Photo by Scout Forbes.)

Monopod Rest

Materials
- One 24-inch length of 1/2-inch diameter pipe (The length will vary depending on the shooter)
- Two 3-inch lengths of 1/2-inch diameter pipe
- Two 1/2-inch diameter 90-degree elbows
- One 1/2-inch diameter T-connector
- Three 1/2-inch diameter end caps
- Foam rubber
- Duct tape
- One large nail
- PVC cement

Instructions:

Step 1
Attach the T-connector to the top of the 24-inch pipe.

Step 2
Attach the elbows to each end of the T-connector, then insert the 3-inch pipes into the ends of the elbows and cap them.

Step 3
Drill a hole through the remaining end cap and insert the nail. Attach this cap to the bottom of the monopod.

Step 4
Wrap foam rubber around the top of the rest to protect your gun. Secure with duct tape.

Since this will more than likely not be taken apart for any reason, cement the project when finished.

Cross-Stick Rest

Tom Forbes takes aim with the help of a cross-stick shooting rest which — unlike the ones used by Buffalo Bill Cody — is made of PVC pipe. (Photo by Scout Forbes.)

Materials:
- Two 36-inch lengths of 1/2-inch diameter pipe
- Four 1/2-inch diameter end caps
- One bolt with nut
- Two large nails
- One heavy-duty rubber band

Instructions:

Step 1
Stand the two 36-inch pieces side-by-side and slip a rubber band over them. Then either kneel or sit behind the pipes and adjust the height of the rubber band so the pipes cross at a height that will put your rifle in a comfortable position.

Step 2
With the height determined, mark the intersection of the two pipes and drill a hole through both of them.

Step 3

Insert the bolt into the holes and snug it up. The wing nut will allow you to adjust the height of the rest by spreading the bases of the pipes.

Step 4

Place an end cap on the top of each pipe, then drill holes through the other two end caps. Insert a nail into each one and snap them on the bottoms of the pipes.

Portable Empty Brass Catcher

If you own a semi-auto firearm and save your brass, you will appreciate the time this device can save you on your hands and knees. Just set it back away from your firearm and it will catch the expended cartridges as they are ejected.

This handy brass catcher is adjustable to accommodate different shooting stances. (Photo by Scout Forbes.)

Materials:
• One 3-foot length of 3/4-inch diameter pipe
• Three 18-inch lengths of 3/4-inch diameter pipe
• Six 14-inch lengths of 3/4-inch diameter pipe
• Two 7-inch lengths of 3/4-inch diameter pipe

- Two 3/4-inch diameter T-connectors
- Four 3/4-inch diameter 90-degree elbows
- Two 3/4-inch diameter three-way 90-degree elbows
- Four 3/4-inch diameter end caps
- One 18-inch-square mesh laundry bag

Instructions:

Step 1

Attach the two 7-inch pipes to the side openings of a T-connector. Then place an elbow on the open end of each 7-inch pipe.

Step 2

Insert an 18-inch pipe into the open end of each elbow, and then place an elbow on each of these open ends. Now complete the square by connecting the elbows with the remaining 18-inch pipe.

Step 3

Slide the top of the 3-foot pipe into the bottom of the T-connector at the base of the square. Add the second T-connector to the bottom of the 3-foot pipe. Insert two of the 14-inch pipes into the sides of the T-connector.

Step 4

Attach the 3-way elbows to the 14-inch pipes and then make the legs by attaching the other four 14-inch pipes to the remaining openings. Add end caps.

Step 5

Place the open end of the laundry bag around the square and tighten the drawstring at the top.

To help stabilize the brass catcher, put some sand or lead shot in the legs. Also, you can use several different heights of PVC pipe to accommodate different shooting positions, such as standing, kneeling, or even prone.

Chapter 9

Weapons

Having a passion for implements of destruction, I thought it only fitting to share some of the things I have made over the years. Some are for training purposes while others are the real deal. Let's start with the training weapons

Nunchakus

As most who have tried to master the nunchakus can testify to, learning can be somewhat painful. By making a set out of PVC pipe you can save yourself a lot of bruises.

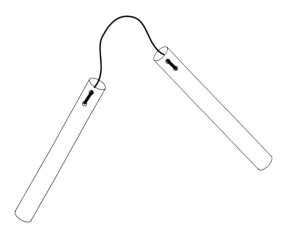

Materials:
- Two 12-inch lengths of 1/2- or 1-inch diameter pipe
- Spray foam insulation
- 8 inches of para cord

Instructions:

Step 1
Drill two holes all the way through each pipe. The first hole should be 1/4-inch from the top and the next one inch down from the first.

Step 2
Spray the foam into each pipe starting at the bottom of the second hole. Once it has set up, trim off the excess.

Step 3

Run the para cord through the top and bottom holes of both pipes.

Step 4

Knot the ends of the cord at the bottom holes, heating the knots with a match or a lighter to secure them.

Fighting Staff/Baton

The construction for both of these items is basically the same, the only difference being the length of the pipe.

Training in the martial arts can be made decidedly less painful by using safely padded mock-weapons made of PVC pipe. Here, author Tom Forbes displays a fighting staff and a baton made of the lightweight material. (Photos by Scout Forbes.)

Materials:
- One 5-foot length of 1-inch diameter pipe
- Two 1-inch diameter end caps
- One 5-foot piece of pipe insulation
- Spray foam insulation
- Para cord (optional for baton)

Instructions:

Step 1

Spray the foam insulation into the pipe. Once this has set up, trim off the excess.

Step 2

Slip the pipe insulation over the staff and cement the end caps on.

The process is the same for making a training baton. One added feature would be to drill a hole through the pipe about 8 inches from the end and run a para cord lanyard through it.

Pugil Sticks

No movie or story about boot camp is complete without mentioning pugil-stick fighting—the army's favorite method for releasing basic survival instincts. Remember though, if you make one you will have to make another—otherwise it's just no fun! As with all mock weapons, it is important to wear proper protective clothing and headgear.

Materials:
- One 5-foot length of 1-inch diameter pipe
- Two 1-inch diameter end caps
- Three 1-foot pieces of pipe insulation or padding from a weight bar
- Two 5-foot by 7-inch sections of 5/8-inch thick foam rubber
- Duct tape
- One can spray foam insulation

Instructions:

Step 1
Spray the foam insulation into the pipe and trim off the excess when it sets up.

Step 2
Slip the three pieces of pipe insulation over the pipe until the

middle piece is centered. Slide the other two pieces so there is about 5 inches of exposed pipe on each side of the middle piece. If you'll be wearing protective gloves, allow for more exposed pipe. Then cement on the end caps.

Step 3

Place the top edge of the foam rubber flush with the end cap and secure it with duct tape its entire width.

Step 4

Wrap the mat around the pipe. When this is complete, anchor the loose end with duct tape and tape all the way around the mat. Repeat the process on the other end and you are done. This should be the bare minimum of padding. Don't be afraid to add more if needed.

Spear

Having a curiosity about spears, I thought it would be kind of neat to have a javelin around the house—to experiment with, or maybe have just in case the Romans should decide to attack. I searched high and low but was unable to find one, so it was time to get creative and build one out of PVC pipe. With that accomplished, I thought, "Why not a real deal spear?" Here is what I came up with.

Materials:
- One 5-foot length of 1/2-inch diameter pipe
- Spray foam
- One handmade spear point with 1/2-inch diameter tang.
- 18 inches of para cord (optional)

Instructions:

Step 1
Drill one or two holes in the pipe. I'm going to leave the distance apart up to you because the tang of your blade will determine the location of the holes.

Step 2
Insert the blade and line up the tang hole with the holes drilled in the pipe. Then secure the blade using either rivets or small nuts and bolts.

Step 3 (optional)

Drill another hole through the pipe (just ahead of the center balance point) and secure a para cord handle by wrapping it around the pipe. Then knot it and make a lanyard out of the excess cord.

Step 4

Spray the foam insulation into the pipe. Once it has set up trim off the excess. Add an end cap if desired.

Important: This is not a toy and must be treated as what it is—a weapon.

Blowgun

Blowguns have always intrigued me, and I thought I might buy one someday. Then I had the opportunity to get to know Mike Janich, author of "Blowguns: The Breath of Death," available from Paladin Press. He suggested that I do one for this book. This one is by no means as intricate as some of his, but it works. Darts can be purchased from sporting goods stores or by mail order. Or you could get Mike's book and learn how to make some downright nasty darts yourself.

Materials:
• One 4-foot length of 1/2-inch diameter CPVC pipe.
• One 2-inch length of 3/4-inch diameter CPVC pipe.
• Duct tape

Instructions:

Step 1
Using a drill, X-Acto knife, or hobby tool, countersink the breech end of the 4-foot pipe. Beveling this edge will help to channel the air when blown through and will allow the dart to slide in more easily.

Step 2
Begin wrapping duct tape around the breech end of the pipe.

When it is thick enough to provide a friction-fit for the 2-inch pipe, slide it over the end and tape it in place.

Important: This is not a toy and should be used with caution.

Chapter 10

Miscellaneous

After constructing the PVC designs in this book, you may start looking around and thinking of other projects that would be useful in your hobbies and outdoors pursuits. Be creative. PVC is so inexpensive that experimenting with different designs is very affordable.

Meanwhile, here are a few more things you can make out of PVC.

Animal Control Stick

Actually, the name sounds more vicious than it really is. This stick allows you to place a snare around an animal's head and control it without exposing yourself to possible danger. It's real handy to have around the farm or garage for removing unwanted critters.

Materials:
- One 5-foot length of 1-inch diameter pipe
- Two 1-inch diameter end caps
- 14 feet of heavy wire or light cable.
- Two cable ends

Instructions:

Step 1
Drill two holes into each end cap big enough for the cable to pass through easily.

Step 2
Run the cable through the holes of one cap, creating a small loop on the outside of the cap. Drop the cable into the pipe so the loose ends are protruding.

Step 3

Cement the cap with the loop onto the pipe. Run the loose ends through the other cap, and cement it to the bottom of the pipe.

Step 4

Clamp a cable end onto one of the loose ends of the cable at the bottom of the stick and pull the opposite end of the cable tight. Clamp the second cable end at the top of the stick, on the cable that will form the fixed end of the loop.

How much cable you feed back through the pipe will determine the size of the loop for snaring the animal's head. Pulling the cable back through will tighten the loop.

Boot Dryer

If you spend any time outdoors, you know how uncomfortable wet shoes or boots can be, especially in cold weather. The PVC boot dryer can help. The secret is to let air circulate throughout the boot, not just the tops. To help speed drying, place the boot dryer in front of a fan so that the air blows up the PVC pipes into the boots.

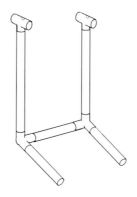

Materials:
- Two 18-inch lengths of 1-inch diameter pipe
- Three 8-inch lengths of 1-inch diameter pipe
- Two 1-inch diameter three-way 90-degree elbows
- Two 1-inch diameter T-connectors

Instructions:

Step 1
Insert the 18-inch pipes into the top openings of the elbows.

Step 2
Connect the elbows with an 8-inch pipe. Insert the remain-

ing two 8-inch pipes into the open ends of the elbows to make the feet.

Step 3

Drill a 1-inch hole in the top of the T-connectors. Then, attach them to the now upright 18-inch pipes.

Caching Supplies and Documents

PVC seems tailor-made for caching supplies and storing documents, pictures, and posters. Many schools and organizations use PVC pipe for time capsules; it's great for storing ammunition and firearms; and it also works well for short-term storage of food items. When caching items in this manner, you should stick with dry goods or items not sensitive to temperature.

The materials and instructions are pretty basic—determine the size of pipe that you need, place some desiccant packets in it and cap both ends.